Marie-Josée Thibault

I Am the Heart of the Rose

St Therese of Lisieux Speaks - Book 1
I Am the Heart of the Rose

Published by Abba Books LLC
abbabooksllc@gmail.com
Copyright © 2023 Marie-Josée Thibault

All Rights Reserved

No part of this publication may be reproduced, distributed, or transmitted in any form or by any means, including photocopying, recording, or other electronic or mechanical methods, without the prior written permission of the publisher.

First Edition, 2023
Designed and Edited by Abba Books LLC
ISBN: 978-1-7377418-6-2

Abba Books LLC
34972 Newark Blvd, #441
Newark, CA 94560

www.abbamyfatheriloveyou.com
https://www.facebook.com/AbbaILoveYouBooks/

Thy Peace on Earth must be achieved. No light, no litany must be spared to honor Thy Grace.
-Saint Paul

CONTENT

Pref ——— V
Ch1 ——— 1
Ch2 ——— 3
Ch3 ——— 5
Ch4 ——— 9
Ch5 ——— 11
Ch6 ——— 15
Ch7 ——— 17
Ch8 ——— 21
Ch9 ——— 25
Ch10 ——— 29
Ch11 ——— 33
Ch12 ——— 37
Ch13 ——— 39
Ch14 ——— 41

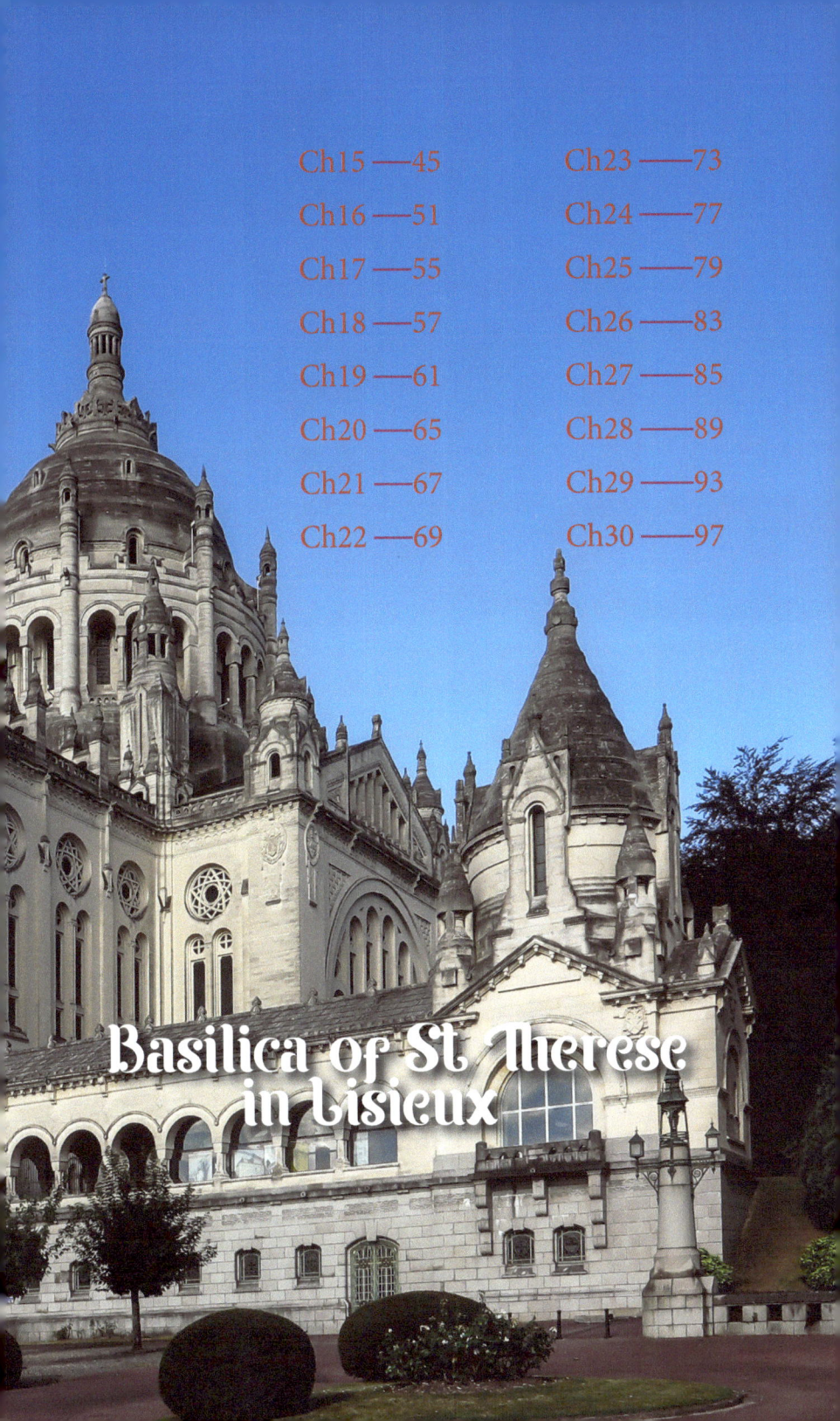

Ch15 —— 45
Ch16 —— 51
Ch17 —— 55
Ch18 —— 57
Ch19 —— 61
Ch20 —— 65
Ch21 —— 67
Ch22 —— 69

Ch23 —— 73
Ch24 —— 77
Ch25 —— 79
Ch26 —— 83
Ch27 —— 85
Ch28 —— 89
Ch29 —— 93
Ch30 —— 97

Basilica of St Therese in Lisieux

Preface

I welcome you, dear little soul, to a world oozing with love, tenderness, gentleness, and—above all—miracles! Enter the extraordinary world that Saint Therese of Lisieux inhabits, and come live with her morning, afternoon, and night while enjoying her touch from Heaven! She loves to shower you with graces and roses from Heaven.

When Therese visits me, she runs toward me and hugs me like she's my big sister, and she smells like a million roses. She is so genuinely loving!

As you read this book, Therese will be standing next to you, and she says so in her book, and it is the truth, as she reports this to me often. By the end of this book, you will believe me.

Therese, I love you!

Marie-Josée

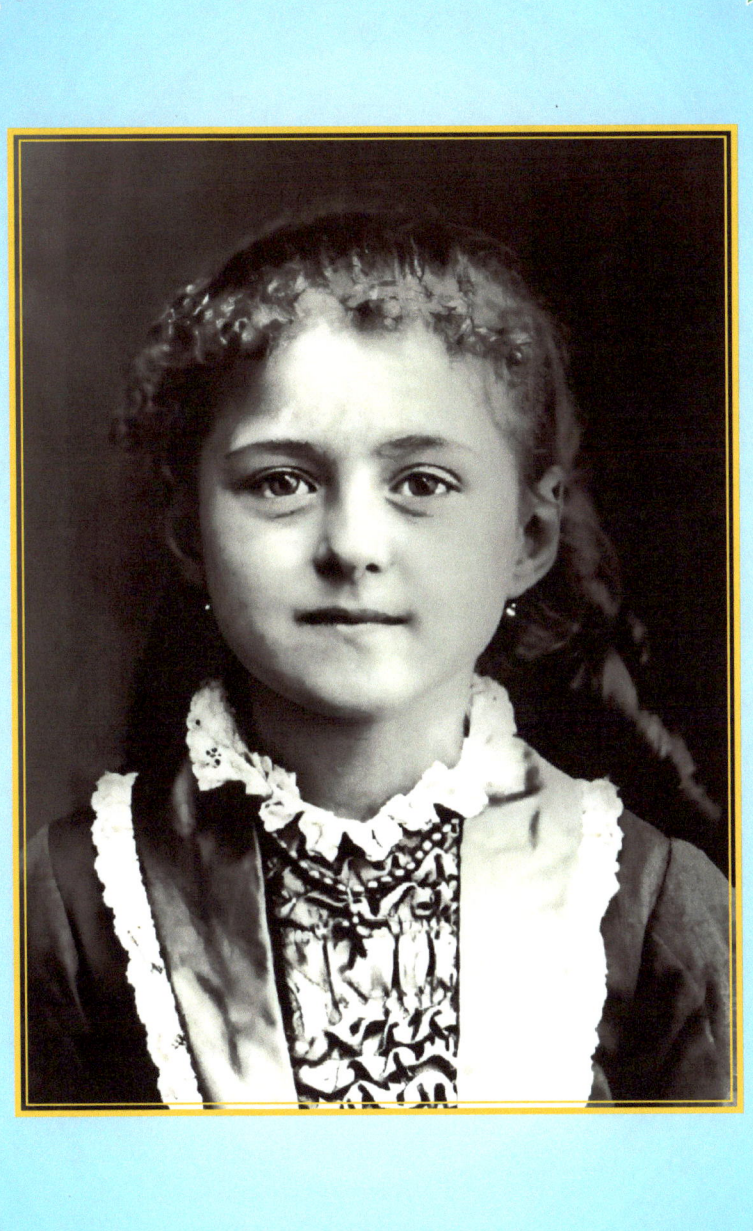

FREE DOWNLOAD

Get your free copy of :
"Saint Padre Pio Speaks: Book 1" when you sign up to the author's VIP mailing list! Get started here:

www.abbamyfatheriloveyou.com

Chapter One

My friends, my children, my brothers and sisters, all my Loves on earth; I am so delighted to speak to you today! My heart pours forth the plenitude of Divine Love in your human hearts in order to make them beautiful, grand, and full of tenderness for those around you.

Yes, I wish to speak to you today of the Heavens through this dictation given to the essence of Saint Paul on earth, Marie-Josée Thibault. I am grateful to this beautiful soul for her devotion to me, to the heavenly court surrounding her, and to Christ Jesus our Lord and our God, One in the Holy Trinity.

I wish to speak to you about Love, the Divine Love that heals everything and forgives everything, the Divine Love enclosed in every rose where I also dwell... For I am the Heart of every rose living on earth. Amen. Alleluia!

Chapter Two

My children of Love, listen to me well. I am in Heaven, and as promised before my physical death, I want to spend my Heaven doing good on earth.

What a joy to live in Paradise! What a delight to behold the Gentle Face of God the Father Almighty! Such gladness to be very close by and to embrace my Love, Christ Jesus, my Savior and my God! So exquisite is living among the Angels of God and the other Saints in Paradise! The beatitudes of the Kingdom of Heaven are true and more beautiful than your mind can imagine!

I love you, and I invite you to join us here in Paradise, and to live with me and all the inhabitants of the Kingdom of God, in the happiness of Love and for Eternity! Amen!

Marie-Josée Thibault

Chapter Three

My children of Love, I am concerned about the state of disgrace of your souls. Awaken now!

Why so much bitterness and sadness? Why so much resentment toward others? Why so much anger vis-à-vis those who disappoint you or persecute you?

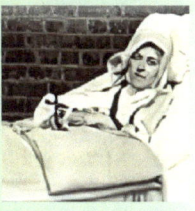

Life on earth (I remember it) is full of obstacles to overcome, chosen with care and Love by God the Father Almighty, in order to enable us to prove our faith in Him, our strength and our courage, our perseverance, and our hope.

Why turn your back on God when God Himself is the Only One Who can really help you in your adversity? He is responsible for setting these tests and tribulations in your life and He is also responsible if these tests and tribulations are removed, according to the extent of your spiritual work.

Why hesitate to grow your faith? Why delay praying, attending Mass,

reading the Bible or other works of theological teaching? Why deny God in your life?

I say unto you, I say unto you verily: God the Father Almighty loves you and He decides everything in your life, as well as in the life of His entire Creation. The Might and the Presence of God in everything, through everything, and at all times, cannot be understood by the human intellect. Do not be confused by the error of the human intellect!

Remind yourself, anywhere and at anytime, that God the Father loves you, sees you, and hears you, and decides at every moment of what presents itself on your path: joys or sorrows, consolations or tribulations, acquisitions or losses, successes or defeats, pleasures or pains. Alleluia! Alleluia! Alleluia! Amen!

Chapter Four

My children of Love: Pray! I will never cease to repeat it: Pray! The assistance you are obtaining through your prayers has no limits! Invoke my name, ask my intercession (or of other Saints in Paradise who adore you just as much) before God the Father Almighty, and repeat often, with joy, fervor and hope... Pray!

Say this: "Saint Therese of Lisieux, intercede for me, before God the Father Almighty, for the obtention of [requested favor], by virtue of the Heart of the Rose and by virtue of your gift of Love, through the Holy and Glorious Name of His Beloved Son, our Lord Jesus Christ, and the Immaculate Heart of Mary. Amen. "

I bless you in the Name of the Father, and of the Son, and of the Holy Spirit, and I love you. I am Saint Therese of Lisieux and I love you!

10 Marie-Josée Thibault

Chapter Five

My children of Love, I urge you to go to church and to participate in liturgical meetings much more often. The benefits you will obtain from these intimate reunions with the Lord Jesus our God are more important for the purification of your soul than you can imagine.

In particular, the communion with Christ through the holy Sacrament of the Eucharist will perform miracles regarding the transformation of your heart and will accelerate your return toward the Father Almighty. For the Holy Sacrament of the Eucharist is the most precious gift given by the Father Almighty to all His children, through the mystical and redeeming Body of His Son, Who is truly found in energetic substance within the consecrated Host.

I love you and I hold you in my arms even closer when you are at Mass or in adoration before the Holy

Eucharist or at the moment of Communion.

May this message pierce your heart with the Truth and Love of Christ the King. Amen.

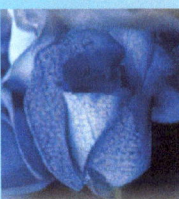

Chapter Six

My beautiful children of Love: I wish to tell you today how much I love you! The immensity of my Love fills the hearts that are opening to me and are receiving me in all my divine plenitude! My Love heals the sick, my Love comforts the afflicted, my Love brings about the solution to every problem you are experiencing, my Love performs miracles that you did not suspect could materialize.

My Love is vaster than everything that stands between you and God the Father, and as a result, my Love can remove all obstacles you encounter on your path!

Alleluia! Alleluia! Alleluia! Blessed is he who receives my Love, for my Love will lead him very rapidly into the Arms of our Loving God! Amen! Alleluia!

Chapter Seven

My very dear children of Love, I wish to tell you today my appreciation for your prayers toward me. Your souls are so beautiful when you pray! I hear and I attend to each and every one of your prayers that are uttered with the intention of my intercession before God the Father Almighty.

I would like to reassure you here that, despite the multitude of prayers destined for me at every second of your temporal dimension, I am able to receive all these messages at once, totally, simultaneously, and with discernment, without losing an iota of the details of your life, and without slowing down or exhausting my zeal before God the Father.

This mystery of the multiplicity of our presence with each one of you, all at once and with an indivisible dedication, is linked to the powers of the Holy Spirit. Do not preoccupy yourself with the operations and intricacies of the Holy Spirit — God the Holy Spirit — One with the Holy Trinity... The human mind will never be able to grasp His ineffable powers.

For the moment, my beloved and adored children, pray! Pray again! For my divine presence is everywhere where my name is spoken or my face imagined—and very often I am there despite the absence of your prayers toward me. For I am Saint Therese of Lisieux and The Almighty has done great things for me! Amen! Alleluia!

Marie-Josée Thibault

Chapter Eigth

My beloved children of the earth in peril: I wish to tell you today to stand firm in your faith in Christ Jesus and to believe in the miracles that the entire Heaven has reserved for you.

Reading this book blessed by God the Father is not a mere chance in your life. I am with you at this moment you are reading this miraculous book; in fact, I have led you so far, with the help of Christ Jesus, my King and my God — my True Love — and a multitude of other servants of God who live in Paradise. I have been observing you for a long time; I have always loved you, and my Love for you has no end and no limit of any kind.

This blessed moment of our spiritual encounter, which takes place now between us through the reading of this sacred book, has been carefully planned with very special attention and total dedication. For your soul is so precious to me, to the Kingdom of God in its entirety and especially to God the

Father Almighty!

The Almighty has commanded me to come to your rescue personally, and it has been my exquisite pleasure and joy to assist you since much longer ago than you can imagine. I love you and I know your life in detail: your joys and your sorrows, your problems, your dreams, your disappointments, and your needs.

Henceforth, I will always be by your side, and I will continue to help you in all your needs, no matter what they are. My ability to perform miracles for you is greater than all the obstacles in your life bound together. In one word, I am your liaison with God, and I will take you directly to Him, in the name of Christ Jesus, our Savior to all, and the Immaculate Heart of Mary, our Divine Mother.

Alleluia! Alleluia! Alleluia! Blessed be God the Father Almighty, for He calls your soul to stand by His side today, close to Him in His Kingdom, and I, Saint Therese of Lisieux, Saint Therese of the Rose, am completely dedicated to you and I love you ! I am

Saint Therese of Lisieux and my heart is filled with Love for you! Love! Amen!

Chapter Nine

My beloved children of the earth: I hold you very close to me at the very depth of my heart!

My heart unfolds from one end to another of planet Earth and converges in a privileged way into the devoted hearts who pray and trust in Christ Jesus, my Love, my Lord and my God, and the Most Blessed Virgin Mary, our Divine Mother to all.

You will be surprised, but above all delighted, to hear me teach you the secret of the rose. The rose is a very elevated plant in its internal vibrations. In fact, the rose holds within itself energies so refined that it communicates with us, here in Paradise. Specifically, the rose—and I wish to specify each of the roses inhabiting the earth—communicate with me, Saint Therese of Lisieux, Servant of God.

Each rose then, within its divine and cosmic plenitude, is endowed with my divine and unique energy, in addition to that of the Holy Trinity. Consequently, every rose inhabiting the earth is impressed within my divine heart; and in return, my divine heart beats, thrives, expands, reaches out for you, finds you, and bonds with you, in all its exquisite and miraculous powers.

For I am the Heart of the Rose, I live and I love you inside each rose, and I speak to you through the rose. I am also in your heart, for I am part of the Kingdom of God, which is found well—nestled at the very depth of each of your human hearts.

Thus, my presence in your life, is found at once in your heart, around you within your etheric energies, and in each of the roses which is heading your way at my command. Do you see?

By the operations of the Holy Spirit, I am able and exalted to be in a position to present you a rose, a bouquet of roses, pictures of roses, a rose fragrance, in order to prove my presence near you.

The rose, my divine heart, and your human heart join altogether in a perfect and luminous current filled with Love, miracles and blessings. I thank God the Father Almighty for so many graces offered to you, my child, and to me, His humble servant.

For I am the Heart of the Rose, and I love you, within the plenitude of God the Father Almighty Who lives in everything. Amen.

St Therese 27

Chapter Ten

My beloved children of the earth, I hold you in my heart, and in the heart of all the roses, for I live in them and I dwell in them — for Eternity. From now on, do not contemplate a rose the same way... Smile to it! Talk to it! Communicate with the rose! And be aware that I live therein!

I receive and I hear all your prayers with a very particular attention, and I hasten before God the Father Almighty to submit your request. My services on your behalf take place with or without the presence of roses. However, remember that we live within energetic dimensions consisting of frequencies and vibrations of all kinds.

Consequently, the presence of roses near you, when you pray for my intercession before God the Father, will amplify the vibrations and the connection being established between us. Furthermore, your intimate and personal emotion, experienced during prayer, will be deeper and richer, and the awaited results will manifest even faster for you, according to the law of attraction.

The magnitude of your faith in God the Father Almighty—and in us, the Saints in Paradise, the Angels of God, who intercede for you—holds a magnetic effect, attracting the intensity and rapidity of miracles performed on your behalf.

Pray hard and with emotion, and all the blessings in your life will appear much faster! Amen!

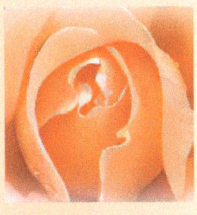

Chapter Eleven

My children of Divine Love, I am in the Heavens at this time I am speaking to you. However, I am delighted to make you become aware that I am also very close to you—just in front of you, in fact—all at once. Your heart extends far beyond what you can imagine, in the energetic dimensions around you.

Since I already exist in your heart (by virtue of the presence in your heart of the Kingdom of Heaven where I live), existing in Paradise in the Heavens and also existing in the Heart of the Rose, you see that I can move as I wish, here and there, all around you, as I so desire, using cosmic rays unknown to men.

Look up before you, at this time, and rest assured that I behold you; I admire your beautiful soul, your beautiful inner Light, made more beautiful and more grand as a result of the Divine Love that I pour forth therein at the very moment you are reading these lines...

I love you! I am the Heart of the

Rose and I am Saint Therese in the Heavens and I love you! Amen!

St Therese 35

Chapter Twelve

My beloved children, I wish to speak to you about my life on earth. I was a little girl like all the other little girls: happy, curious, loving, full of dreams and projects. The difference was buried in my heart: the Lord Jesus Christ had planted a seed that has grown up so fast! He had planted the seed of Life, the exaltation of living with Him, of Love unbounded for my spiritual Husband, even at a young age.

I desired to merge with His Heart of Love, becoming Love, and to love the entire Creation through everything that is Jesus, my Love and my King. My wish was granted. I pray that you also live the sublime rapture of knowing His love and becoming Love! Amen.

Chapter Thirteen

My beloved children, I embrace you with all the Love of Paradise! When I was a child, a teenager and a young woman, I dreamed with hope and trepidation about the day when I would enter into Paradise! This day of ineffable grace granted by God the Father on my little soul has been extraordinary — indeed indescribable through the use of words. Paradise is of such grandeur, such beauty, and such enchantment more exquisite than your wildest dreams! Honor, praise and Love to the Precious Blood of the Lamb of God for allowing my entry into Paradise!

Now it is my turn to allow these treasures from Heaven for you, dear readers. I pray and I will not cease to pray for the salvation of your soul and your glorious entry into Paradise, the Kingdom of Heaven promised to those converted to Christ Jesus, my Love, my Lord and my God! Amen! Alleluia!

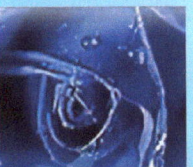

Chapter Fourteen

My beloved children of the earth, I wish to speak to you today about my childhood. Such joy at home! Such Love between my sisters and my beloved father! My mother died when I was at a young age, but her maternal presence was always there. Moreover, my discovery of the Love that the Blessed Virgin Mary carries in Her Heart for all Her children was a blessing from God so to compensate for my mother's painful absence.

Growing up in a religious atmosphere has been a truly unique gift from Heaven when I contemplate the current life contexts in which children are immersed. So much adversity to the spiritual open-mindedness of the child! So many materialistic solicitations from a society destroying itself! My life on earth was bathed in Love, and the promises of Jesus, my little Love of mine, came true beyond my dreams.

I an thankful to Jesus the Christ our Savior for my childhood blessed by

God. I make it my constant prayer to shower you with Divine Love and Divine protection for the rest of your life, and I also keep your family and all those whom you love in my heart.

    Blessed are those invited to Love! Amen!

Chapter Fifteen

My beloved children of the earth, I envelop you with my Love: your thoughts, your emotions, and your actions, henceforth, will be imbued with Love, the Divine Love that overflows into you at this moment, directly into your heart. My Love has the power to heal you, to close the wounds and traumas of the past, to neutralize your negativity, to deepen your faith, to magnify your prayers, to remove obstacles that slow you down or disturb you on your path of return toward God the Father Almighty.

For He Himself has poured forth His Divine Providence on your soul through this miraculous book you are holding in your hands, and by virtue of which my life in Heaven and your life on earth have merged from this moment on — by Love, for Love, through Love, and capable of generating even more Love for the Glory of God the Father. I love you!

Alleluia! Alleluia! Alleluia! Blessed

are those who love, for God—Who is Love—is with them! Amen. Alleluia!

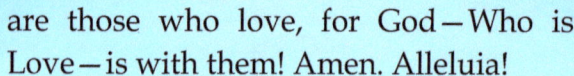

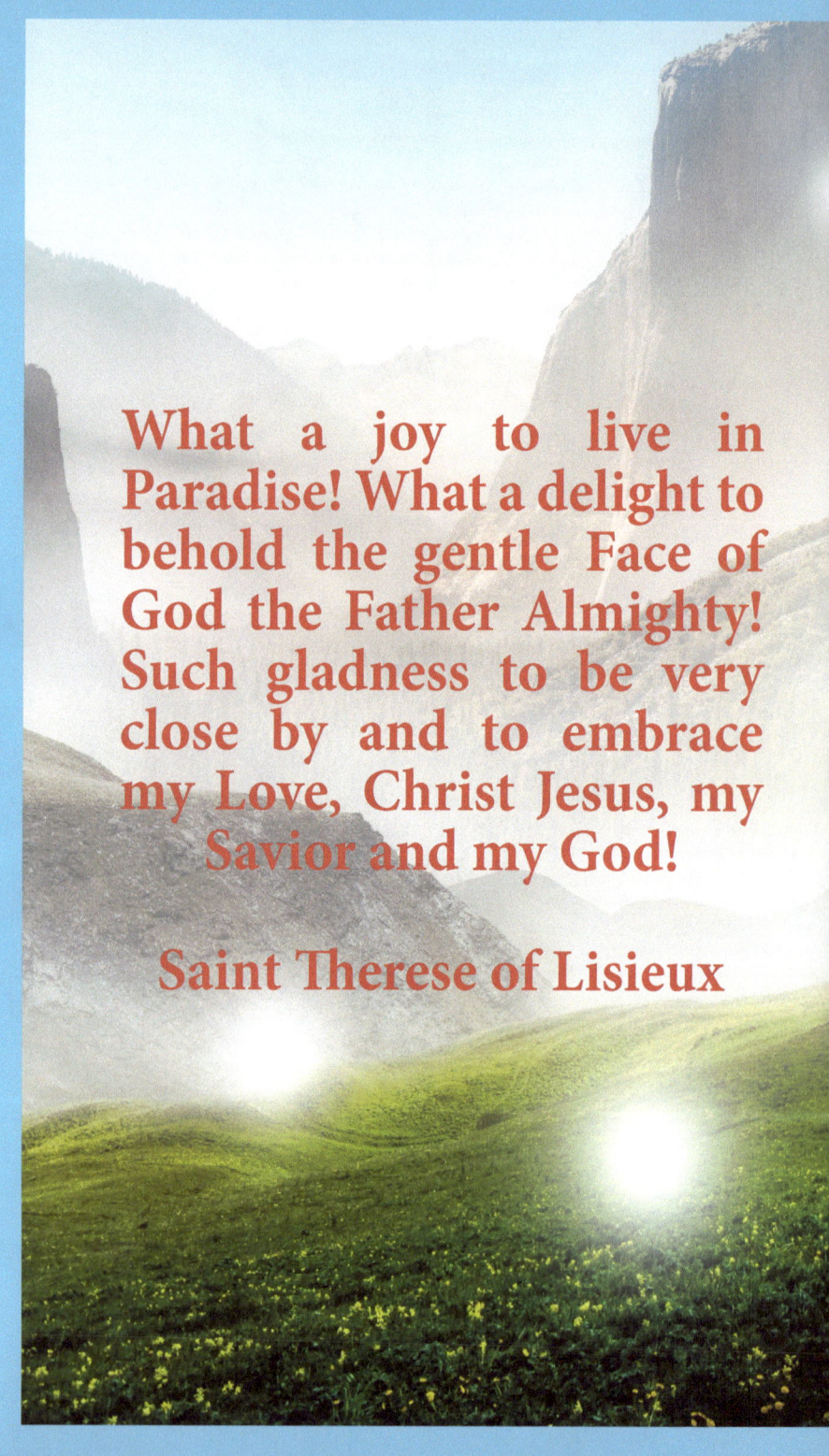

What a joy to live in Paradise! What a delight to behold the gentle Face of God the Father Almighty! Such gladness to be very close by and to embrace my Love, Christ Jesus, my Savior and my God!

Saint Therese of Lisieux

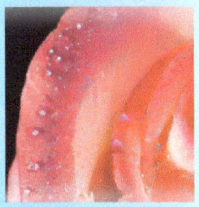

Chapter Sixteen

My dear children of the earth, listen to me well. My earthly life has been a source of suffering during the last period I was alive. However, sources of joy and hope were the result of divine intercessions toward me.

Indeed, the Heavens have opened to me several times during the darkness that was my agony and the physical pain associated with my disease. I saw the Most Blessed Virgin Mary appear before me and she comforted me with a sweetness and tenderness that cannot exist on earth. I was in a state of mystical enchantment and rapture never experienced before in my life. Her exquisite Beauty, Her Light, and Her Love have helped my healing and my redemption in an accelerated way for my soul thirsty for Paradise.

My Divine Mother, the Most Blessed Virgin Mary, whom I adore and honor today in your behalf, appeared to me several times before my physical death, and Her divine and miraculous intercession has assured the transformation of my human heart into a divine heart.

Pray often to the most Holy, the most glorious Blessed Virgin Mary, our Mother to us all, the true source of Divine Love!

I am so happy to be able to speak to you now and to share with you all the Love of Paradise that I carry in my Heart so vast. Love! Joy! Peace! I bless you in the Name of the Father, and of the Son, and of the Holy Spirit. I love you. I am Saint Therese of the Rose. Amen. Alleluia!

Chapter Seventeen

My dear beloved children, I am in the Heavens with the celestial court surrounding Marie-Josee, the essence of Saint Paul, the one taking this dictation, at this very moment I am speaking to her.

I love Marie-Josée and I wish to infuse the plénitude of my Love into her heart, which is opening more and more to Divine Love, to pure Love, to the celestial Love originating from God the Father Almighty.

Similarly, I wish to infuse the plenitude of my Love into your heart, dear reader, so to bring you safely to the Kingdom of Heaven where I live, and to receive you at its doors, with joy and elation, at the moment of the passage that is death.

Continue reading this book, my beautiful child, for I am with you — yes, you — at this precise second. I love you and this is Therese of Lisieux who is speaking to you, my beloved child. Amen.

Marie-Josée Thibault

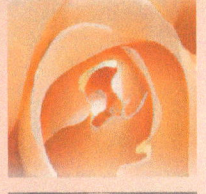

Chapter Eighteen

My beloved children, come into my arms now! I have waited for this moment blessed by God for so long, despite my spiritual closeness with you, and this, independantly from your perception of my presence near you. My heart of Love could not wait another second to hold you in my arms!

My Love generates even more Love when a soul receives my heart filled with the treasures of Heaven for you! Such is the key of Love: Love thrives and multiplies when it flows into a heart that wishes Love! And these little miracles of Love spread and soon will flood planet Earth with more Love than darkness, thus contributing to the God's Great Plan of Salvation, which is based solely on Love, by Love, and for Love, so that one day, only Love will live and reign on earth.

Alleluia! Alleluia! Alleluia! Blessed is he who becomes Love, for I—Saint

Therese of Lisieux—will be Love with him, world without end. Amen.

Marie-Josée Thibault

Chapter Nineteen

My beloved children of the earth, all is never lost. Do not be afraid! Pray and hope! The powers of the Saints to assist you in your prayers are limitless!

Simply say: "Saint Therese of Lisieux, Saint Therese of the Rose, intercede for me, before God the Father Almighty, for the obtention of [requested favor], by virtue of the Heart of the Rose and by virtue of your gift of Love, through the Holy and Glorious Name of our Lord Jesus Christ and the Immaculate Heart of Mary. Amen. "

Thanks to this call, I hurry at your service, I offer my help in your needs, I hasten to bring you the solution to the problems you are exposing to me. Nothing escapes my attention with regard to your life and your needs, and nothing is too sizeable for me that I cannot do for you. Ask and you shall receive!

Alleluia! Alleluia! Alleluia! Blessed is he who prays to God the Father and asks for the intercession of the Saints in Paradise, for God the Father Himself in this rejoices. Amen. Alleluia!

Chapter Twenty

My beloved children, always be with gladness in the heart! If you only knew the joy and Love that radiates from the perfect and Light-resplendent Face of our Beautiful Jesus!

Jesus Christ, my Love, my Savior and my God, is Pure Love, Pure Joy, Pure Peace. The smile He has at this very moment—since I am watching Him—is the most beautiful in the world. For at this very moment, my dear reader, Christ Jesus and I are with you, and we cannot contain our pleasure and our joy at beholding you, my beautiful soul, for we are actively preparing your royal entrance into Paradise. Such joy in the Heart of Christ Jesus Who has been awaiting you for so long!

Say Yes to Jesus now! Say Yes to Jesus again and say: Jesus, I love You! For, Jesus, I believe in You! Amen. Alleluia!

Chapter Twenty-One

My beloved children, I rejoice in your spiritual progress. Shortly, I will be able to interact even more in your life and fill you with the graces of Heaven. Nothing is impossible to me! My Love for you, my Love for Jesus, my Love for God the Father, are ineffable and are cosmic forces capable of performing miracles for you, even more powerful and meaningful that the human mind can conceive.

For the salvation of your soul is what matters to me at the highest point; and my Love holds the promise of your entrance into the Kingdom of God awaiting you. Glory to God in the highest Heaven and peace on earth to men of good will. Amen. Alleluia!

Chapter Twenty-Two

My beloved children of the earth, always remain in my arms when fear seizes you! Come and take refuge here, close by my heart filled with Love for you, and I shall comfort you personally, I will give you the solution to the problems beseting you, and I will cure you in all aspects of your body.

The Heavens hold the solution to every problem you will encounter in your life. In fact, our divine intervention represents the only escape route for you, dear people of the earth, due to the gravity of offenses committed and the immensity of the debt to God of humanity in general. Do not be afraid! I am here with you now and for the rest of your life—and beyond.

I will assist you in overcoming all the obstacles you must go through on your path of return toward God. For there is no other path to take than the one leading into the loving Arms of

God, our Father Creator.

I love you.

Amen. So be it.

Chapter Twenty-Three

My beloved children, I am pleased to speak to you today about my heart. My human heart has been transformed into a divine Heart by the grace of God the Father Almighty, Who loves all His children equally. My divine Heart, similar to that of Christ Jesus, my King and my Love, beats only for you, dear reader, my child chosen by God. Yes, dear child of Love, Love itself, being God, has chosen you for His Kingdom of Heaven, and He has assigned your soul to my divine Heart. Do you see?

My heart opens very wide for all the children whom God the Father Almighty takes pleasure in including in His Great Plan of Salvation. Love God, talk to Him, ask His forgiveness for sins committed against Him and against your fellowmen, and God will continue to pour forth His graces of Love and Mercy into your life.

The proof? You are reading this

book blessed by God, and I am speaking to you here and now, and above all, I assist you and accompany you every day of your life, and I will wait for you with open arms and a heart beating with joy and excitement during your grand entrance into Paradise.

For my divine Heart loves you and beats only for you! By the grace and the operations of the Holy Spirit Who performs the miracle of the multiplicity of my presence, rest assured that each and every one of my children on earth is unique and indispensable to me, despite the inconceivability of this miracle of Love.

For my Love is indivisible and total, it is miraculous and transcendent, it is eternal and marvellous, by the grace of God Who loves you all equally. Amen. Alleluia!

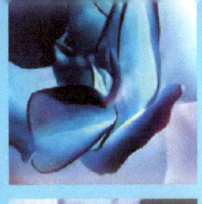

Chapter Twenty-Four

My beloved children of the earth, I bless you, in the Name of the Father, and of the Son, and of the Holy Spirit. My blessing upon you, at this point in your life, is the vehicle of Love, Peace, and Life in Christ Jesus, my Love and my King.

Rejoice! For myself, Saint Therese of Lisieux, the Heart of the Rose, the Grace of Love in the Heavens, has entered your life, forever and ever, world without end. I give thanks to God the Loving Father for so much mercy granted to your soul, so small and so beautiful in my arms...

Alleluia! Alleluia! Alleluia! Blessed is the reader of this book blessed by God, for God Himself embraces you today with all His fatherly Love, which He had reserved for you, little soul adored by us all! Amen. Alleluia!

Chapter Twenty-Five

My beloved children of the earth, give me the pleasure of hearing your voice! Your prayers enchant me, even the simplest and smallest, from you, dear reader, little soul in need. Always remain in a state of reverence before God, for we can hear each and every prayer you make, as well as what you say internally that is not pronounced.

Yes, we can hear everything you say in your heart, no matter if these words are destined to us. Your inner conversations with yourself, your arguments of justification, your comments about your interactions with other people, your plans and strategies for the future, large and small dramas that you stage on the theater of your heart: we hear everything.

Consequently, dear soul whom I carry in my heart, be reverential before the divinity, at all times and everywhere, for each of your thoughts, emotions and actions are known to us—and of God inevitably! Monitor your inner conversation; do not fall into vain and useless rambling as a result of internal reflections that lead nowhere.

Pray! Instead of wasting your time about a ridiculous inner drama, pray! And pray again! These internal requests and petitions are much more productive and meritorious that you can imagine! And God the Father will take pleasure in beholding your soul that prays! Amen. Alleluia!

Chapter Twenty-Six

My children, be firm in your faith in the Lord Jesus Christ. No matter what happens in your life, trust in Him! As you move closer to Him, He moves closer to you, and He will be your Fortress through all the obstacles in your life.

Christ Jesus, my Lord and my King, is the Master of the world! He is capable of all miracles for you, even the most unimaginable! Let Him step into your life and shower you with the grace and blessings of Heavens. My intercession in this regard is ongoing for you so that you can live with Him — My Jesus, my Heart, and my Joy — as soon as possible. Alleluia! Alleluia! Alleluia!

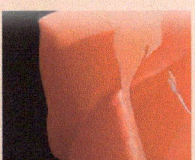

Chapter Twenty-Seven

My beloved children of the earth, be very clear here that this message comes directly from the Heavens. The divine and personal revelations received by Marie-Josée Thibault are genuine, true, powerful, and sanctioned by God the Father Himself, Who loves you so much. He has allowed you to read this book today in order to obtain the salvation of your soul, through my divine and unique intercession.

I, Saint Therese of Lisieux, the Heart of the Rose, have been assigned by God Himself as a benevolent Saint responsible for the future of your soul. My joy is boundless to be able to assist you in what concerns the fundamental question of your entire life: what will happen to your soul after the passage that is death?

Verily, verily, I say unto you, take care of your soul now, before it is too late. I will make every effort and all the prayers necessary to ensure the salvation of your soul.

Alleluia! Alleluia! Alleluia! Blessed are the elect of my divine Heart, for I, Saint Therese of Lisieux, the Heart of the Rose, will take you directly to Paradise with the Angels of God, Christ Jesus, and the Most Blessed Virgin Mary! Amen. Alleluia!

Chapter Twenty-Eight

My children, rejoice and be glad, for the Kingdom of God awaits you after the passage that is death!

I am personally taking charge of the cleansing of your soul and the elimination of the obstacles impeding your spiritual growth at this point in your life. Other Saints also speak through the essence of Saint Paul on earth, Marie-Josée Thibault; their powers of intercession before God are as miraculous as mine.

What is the difference between me and the other Saints in Paradise? None. We have all become Christic Energy. We are at the image of Christ in the Eyes of God, for we have imitated Christ during our life on earth. This means that Christ Jesus is the Christ Most High, the most elevated Being in the Creation, our Master and King. We form but One, One Body in Christ, by virtue of the Holy Spirit and in the glory of God the Father, whom we adore. Alleluia!

Read all the books dictated to the essence of Saint Paul on earth, Marie-Josée, and follow your emotions. I am here to help you for the rest of your life—and beyond. And after reading the other books dictated to Marie-Josée, other Saints in Paradise also will accompany you during your journey.

Pray to me and pray to other Saints in Paradise, alternatively, according to the emotions of your heart, several times a day. Pray! Pray! Pray! Our approach (that is to say each and every Saint in Paradise) is different and unique; however, our goal is the same: your royal entry into the Kingdom of Heaven.

There is no competition between us (there is no darkness here) for we, the Saints in Paradise, form but One, One Body in Christ. Pray as often as possible, to the greatest possible number of Saints Who are opening your heart to the treasures of Paradise, and we will all be enchanted to wait for you with open arms after the passage that is death. We are all here for you, dear reader, and we love you perfectly and equally, completely and eternally, world without end. Amen. Alleluia!

Chapter Twenty-Nine

My beloved children, I am infinitely grateful for all the prayers intended for me all around the world. I hear all the prayers destined for my intercession and I execute all the requested prayers before God immediately, with zeal and Love. What joy in Paradise when the prayers of human hearts on earth reach us!

Your Guardian Angel, Who is always with you and Who is of incomparable divine benevolence, hastens to intensify efforts for you so, that your prayers and requests might be amplified and effective before God. Your Guardian Angel adores you and He often communicates with us (the Saints in Paradise) about what concerns the details of your life, your progress, your delays, the obstacles you encounter.

Talk often to your Guardian Angel; ask Him to pray for you before God the Father Almighty, ask Him to accelerate your spiritual growth, and He will be exalted to do everything possible, on earth as in Heaven, in order to submit to God your soul made as beautiful and exquisite as a precious stone. For your Guardian Angel is devoted to you completely; He is your companion for life and your direct liaison with God.

Alleluia! Alleluia! Alleluia! Blessed is he who prays to his Guardian Angel, for God Himself in this rejoices! Amen. Alleluia!

Chapter Thirty

My children, my beloved children, I am with you until the end of times — and beyond. My life has joined with yours through the Infinite Mercy of God the Father Almighty. I am thankful to the Holy Trinity, world without end.

I embrace you and give you all the Love my holy and divine Heart contains, and my Love will guide you to Paradise where I am.

I am the Heart of the Rose and I am Saint Therese of Lisieux in the Heavens.

I bless you in the Name of the Father, and of the Son, and of the Holy Spirit. Amen. Alleluia!

I love you.

Therese

Afterword

Therese of Lisieux has officially, completely, perfectly, and eternally entered your life. This blessing has been granted by the Mercy and Love of God the Father Almighty and through the heart of Jesus, our King and Savior.

Glory be to God in the Highest Heaven!

Marie-Josée

About the Author

Marie-Josée Thibault's life is in no way similar to yours. When she wakes, the saints of Heaven visit her, talk to her, teach her, and pray intensely with her. When such mystical sessions draw to a close, she greets with great respect and deep reverence the Masters of the Heavenly Court. This servant of the Lord spends the rest of the day in the company of her guardian angel, who continues her spiritual education and ceaselessly protects her from the perils of this fallen world.

Bestowed by the Heavenly Father, her gifts of clairvoyance and clairaudience allow her to remain in continuous contact with the supernatural dimension juxtaposed with ours, where the soul is born of the Spirit through Jesus and Mary. She prays that, one day soon, the entire human race will give glory to the Father, the Son, and the Holy Spirit.

Saint Padre Pio Speaks:
Book 1
Abba, Your Father, Speaks:
Book I
Abba, Your Father, Speaks:
Book II
Angel Gabriel Speaks:
Book 1
Dear Humanity: Book 1
Dear Humanity: Book 2

Abso by Author

FREE DOWNLOAD

Get your free copy of : "Saint Padre Pio Speaks: Book 1" when you sign up to the author's VIP mailing list! Get started here:

www.abbamyfatheriloveyou.com

Marie-Josée Thibault

www.ingramcontent.com/pod-product-compliance
Lightning Source LLC
Chambersburg PA
CBHW041802160426
43191CB00001B/7